ACT NOW

How Successful Consultants
Thrive During Chaos and
Uncertainty

By Michael Zipursky

If you would like further information about
Consulting Success® or any of our products,
programs, or services please email us at
info@consultingsuccess.com

Library and Archives Canada Cataloguing in
Publication. Zipursky, Michael, author

Consulting Success®/Michael Zipursky
ISBN (e-book) 978-1-7750411-3-9
(paperback) 978-1-7750411-4-6
1. Consulting 2. Marketing. 3. Entrepreneurship

"The future is uncertain but this uncertainty is at the very heart of human creativity."

Ilya Prigogine

Table of Contents

1

The World Has Changed...and It Hasn't

From wars, natural disasters, and global pandemics to business setbacks and personal tragedies, calamity can hit us at many different levels, and whatever form it takes, when trouble strikes, it shakes our confidence. The current crisis of COVID-19 has rocked industries, business owners, and workers all over the world.

As politicians scramble to stave off the worst-case scenario, people from all walks of life are struggling to adjust to quarantines, voluntary self-isolation, "social distancing," panic buying, and an uncertain economic future.

As a consultant, you may be feeling a bit stressed out yourself. All of the stories about shuttered businesses and empty grocery store shelves can certainly induce a certain amount of anxiety. How bad are things going to get? Will you still have clients? Maybe you've already lost many, if not most, of your clients. How can your consultancy survive? You are not alone in asking these questions.

You may already know people who have tested positive for COVID-19, who are currently suffering from the disease, or who have tragically passed away as a result. One of my clients lost a close family member recently. Though he didn't have the disease, he was being hospitalized for another health condition. When the hospital was inundated with people suffering from COVID-19, he was removed from a ventilator so they could give it to another patient.

It's a heartbreaking situation, and these kinds of tragedies are happening to people in many countries right now. Things may get worse before they get better.

However, even when the COVID-19 pandemic settles—and it eventually will—there is always the potential for some other crisis to come along and threaten our sense of stability.

Maybe you're dealing with a business or personal problem that has nothing to do with the pandemic but which has threatened your health, well-being, or economic stability.

The point is, we all deal with times of tremendous instability, and when they happen, they often catch us off-guard. It's natural to be concerned, and under the circumstances, I empathize with anyone who is feeling fearful. Our daily routines have been interrupted, and the status quo has changed.

There is a lot to worry about:

- The future of your business.

- The future of your industry.

- The future of your investments.

- The health and well-being of family and friends.

- Your own health and well-being.

Although alarmism is not all that unusual when it comes to news media stories, you might be wondering if this time they're right. Are things really going to get so much worse that we never fully recover?

To be clear, there's nothing wrong with worrying about difficult circumstances. On the contrary, worry is a normal, even healthy, response for anyone—and it's especially common for entrepreneurs.

If you're not worried right now, you might not be thinking enough about the future of your business. I talk about this at length in my book *The Elite Consulting Mind*, but the essence of my advice is this:

Successful people worry, but they worry well.

What makes worry detrimental is when you spend too much time dwelling on the negative, expecting the worst, and sinking into despair. On the other hand, if you can use your worry to help you stay focused on the things that matter most, then it will serve you well.

Whatever the future holds, the biggest battle in a crisis like this—in *any* crisis, really—is the mental war that we wage. If you can continue to think clearly and strategize well, you will make better decisions to overcome difficult situations, identifying and making the most of great opportunities along the way. In so doing, you can position yourself to manage the hardships and come out the other side further ahead.

To help you do that, I want to share some best practices, mindset shifts, strategies, and concrete actions you can take during these challenging times that will help you weather the storm and, more than that, continue to thrive no matter what.

I hope this book can serve as a guide for anyone facing chaos or uncertainty, particularly if you're feeling overwhelmed and unsure about the future.

Mental Strategies for Trying Times

Here's the reality: chaos is a constant enemy in your mind. It doesn't strike only during a recession, pandemic, or personal crisis, and it doesn't necessarily wait until you're ready for it. At any moment, chaos can cause you to react in ways that hurt your business or cause you to fail to take advantage of growth opportunities.

However, if you can learn to master the chaos within, you will be better prepared to deal with any challenge that life throws at you.

More than that, if you can think clearly in hard times, the challenges presented might become motivating factors in improving yourself and your business in ways you otherwise never would have imagined, inspiring you to get more creative, push harder, plan smarter, and act more boldly.

To begin getting your mind in order, I recommend a few mindset shifts and strategies for trying times:

1) Focus on Opportunities Instead of Setbacks

During difficult times, some of the things you've taken for granted—such as economic opportunities, market trends, client behavior, or ways of doing business—may change or even disappear altogether. When that happens, it can shake you to your core.

In fact, some people never get over it. Instead of adjusting to the changes, they continue to live in the past—still trying to replay their old games and wondering why they can no longer get ahead.

When the world changes, even if some things that you relied on are lost, new opportunities become available.

13

If you can stop focusing on your setbacks and start looking for those new opportunities, you may suddenly find that you can achieve far more than you ever did in the past.

The key is to recognize that there are *always* numerous opportunities. You just have to be open to them, and you have to start *looking*.

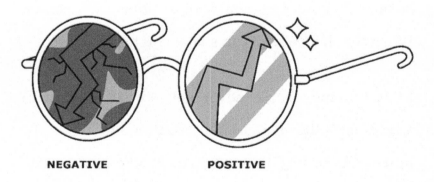

NEGATIVE   POSITIVE

2) Focus on Progress Instead of Problems

When chaos appears, "business as usual" is no longer as easy as it once was. The difficulties can defeat you if you let them, or they can reveal new strengths that you didn't even know you possessed.

Think of it this way: the muscles in your body only get stronger when you work against resistance. Isn't it strange that lifting heavy weights builds even more muscle mass?

The science behind it is called *hypertrophy*. When you put your body through an intense anaerobic exercise, you actually cause damage to your muscle fibers (called *microtrauma*), but as your body recovers from a workout, it begins repairing those damaged muscles.

In the process, white blood cells rush to the injured muscles to reduce inflammation, proteins are released which produce satellite cells, and those satellite cells fuse with existing muscle fibers. This repairs the damage, but it also thickens the muscle fibers and makes them larger and stronger.[1]

It is in the tension, the resistance against an opposing force, that our muscles become stronger. The same is true for the "muscles" of your mind. Treat a time of difficulty as a time to make greater progress in your thinking, learning, and character development.

You might find that you come out the other side a far better, more skilled, and more successful person.

3) Focus on Value Creation

Even in the best of times, most people can't stand a sales pitch. When times are uncertain or scary, their contempt for being sold to only intensifies. Anxious people are more likely to turn off the video, put the

---

[1] Dr. Rachel Tavel, PT, DPT, CSCS, "How You Can Use Hypertrophy to Grow Your Muscles," *Men's Health*, November 21, 2018, https://www.menshealth.com/fitness/a25252586/muscle-hypertrophy/

email in the trash folder, hang up the phone, or slam the door in your face.

However, all people at all times appreciate *value creation*. Whether things are going well or falling apart, if you can provide solutions to their problems, and accelerate results and outcomes they care about, people will listen.

Focus on creating value at all times—even when the future seems bleak—and sales will naturally follow.

By providing value, you expose your clients and potential clients to new ideas and opportunities that they hadn't thought about. Therefore, they will feel less risk—and more confidence—about making an investment, even during times like these, which could result in a new project for you.

We will look at some concrete ways you can do this later in the book.

4) Focus on Gratitude

It's easy to obsess over all of the things we've lost or might lose. In fact, it's natural for a scared mind to play through worst-case scenarios and potential catastrophes over and over again, and it's also natural to feel regret when we miss out on opportunities, lose clients, or experience a decline in revenue.

However, obsessing over the things you've lost or might lose doesn't fix anything. On the contrary, it just might motivate you to make some poor decisions and miss out on even more opportunities.

Instead of thinking about the bad, concentrate on being grateful for what you have. At a bare minimum, chances are you still have access to food, water, electricity, a roof over your head, and a bed to lie in at night. These are things that millions of people around the world don't have, even in the best of times.

Gratitude has a profound impact on your perspective. It enables you to remain positive when others are falling apart, and when you're positive, you can avoid rash decisions and keep moving forward.

As Tony Robbins has said, "Choosing gratitude and appreciation over criticism and negativity leads to attracting more of the things you can appreciate and be grateful for."[2]

This isn't just a platitude. There's actual science behind it. According to *Psychology Today*, studies have shown that grateful people are emotionally healthier, more empathetic, mentally stronger, and more resilient.[3]

---

[2] Team Tony, "Where Focus Goes, Energy Flows," *Tony Robbins*, https://www.tonyrobbins.com/career-business/where-focus-goes-energy-flows/
[3] Amy Morin, "7 Scientifically Proven Benefits of Gratitude," *Psychology Today*, April 3, 2015, https://www.psychologytoday.com/us/blog/what-mentally-strong-people-dont-do/201504/7-scientifically-proven-benefits-gratitude

5) Focus on What You Can Do Right Now

When things are going well, people often assume they're in control of events. "My business is going great. I'm getting more clients and making more money. I must be doing something right," they think. "I've got this all figured out!"

Therefore, when things turn bad, it's understandable that they might wonder if they've lost their touch. They feel defeated and depressed. "What did I do wrong?" they wonder. "What happened to me? I used to be so good at this. When did I lose control?"

The most consistently successful people know that they can't control events. Instead, they work continually toward greater control of their *response* to every event—good or bad.

Whenever they feel fear, anxiety, or uncertainty, they see it as an excellent time to focus all of their attention and energy on making the most of the circumstances. They accept that unpredictable events lie ahead, but they look for the opportunities.

If you can get your mindset right, you can begin to strategize wisely in troubling times. In the next chapter, we'll look at some ways you can begin to get a handle on this.

┌─────┐
│ **2** │
└─────┘

What You Can Control

When I say the biggest battle is your mental war against fear and chaotic thinking, I don't mean to suggest that your problems aren't real.

At the time of writing this book, the current pandemic is a very real problem with potentially devastating real-life consequences for millions of people.

Your health might really be in danger, the health of friends, family, neighbors, and coworkers might be in danger, and the economic fallout from government attempts to contain the spread of the disease are all real. Businesses, even whole industries, have already been seriously impacted.

Nevertheless, we've been here before. COVID-19 isn't the first global pandemic, and it won't be the last. While there are aspects of the current situation that are unique, the same is true of every crisis. That doesn't mean you shouldn't take it seriously.

Take recommended precautions, but don't assume the sky is falling. Whenever a major event impacts world events, there's a pervasive fear that we're entering an unrecoverable economic death spiral, but we've been through this before. In fact, it's old news.

The Market Always Bounces Back

The first stock market crash in history is generally believed to be the bursting of the speculative bubble on Dutch tulips in the 17th century. After prices skyrocketed between 1634 and 1637, speculators cornered the market, buying up all the tulips they could get their hands on.

This, in turn, caused the interest in tulips to wane, and the market crashed. The ripple effect sent the Dutch economy into a tailspin. It must have seemed like the end of the world, economically speaking, but the market recovered.

The first major U.S. stock market crash in 1929 brought the Roaring '20s to an end and ushered in the Great Depression, the worst economic downturn in the history of the industrialized world. Caused by inflated stock prices, reckless speculation, and over-borrowing, the resulting fallout caused widespread panic.

The consequences were devastating. In the immediate aftermath, consumer confidence evaporated, which led to a massive downturn in spending. Production slowed, and by 1932, worldwide gross domestic product (GDP) had fallen by an estimated 15 percent. Unemployment in the U.S. reached 23 percent, and almost half of the banks in the country failed.

Because of global adherence to the gold standard, which created a fixed currency exchange, the economic woes soon spread from the U.S. across North America, into Europe, and throughout the world.[4]

---

[4] History.com editors, "Great Depression History," *History*, https://www.history.com/topics/great-depression/great-depression-history

It must have seemed like the market would never recover. In fact, it took twelve years and a Great Depression, but the stock market *did* recover.

It also recovered from the Dot.com bust of 1999, which was caused by excessive speculation in Internet-related businesses. It recovered after 9/11.

It recovered from the Great Recession of 2008, when the U.S. housing market bubble burst due to an overabundance of subprime loans. Are you seeing a trend?

As this chart makes clear, there have been numerous bear markets just in the last few decades, and the Dow Jones has recovered from all of them.

Bull & Bear Markets

Day of Start	Length (Months)	DOW JONES TR
May 26, 1970	31.6	84.00%
January 11, 1973	20.7	-39.70%
October 3, 1974	73.9	132.90%
November 28, 1980	20.4	-12.80%
August 12, 1982	60.4	337.00%
August 25, 1987	3.3	-34.70%
December 4, 1987	31.4	88.70%
July 16, 1990	2.9	-20.30%
October 11, 1990	113.4	492.20%
March 24, 2000	30.5	-31.40%
October 9, 2002	60.0	117.70%
October 9, 2007	17.0	-51.80%
March 9, 2009	131.4	491.90%
February 19, 2020	1.2	-27.60%

0.00%   200.00%   400.00%

Source: S&P 500 Dow Jones Indices as of market close on March 25, 2020

The point is, we've been here before, and we'll probably be here again. When trouble of any kind hits the economy, some see only doom and gloom. They focus on the current loss and project that into the future, expecting the worst and responding accordingly—typically, by freezing up and failing to respond at all.

It's true that the markets historically pull back in times of disruption and crisis, but they almost always recover the losses—and then some—in the years that follow. With the right mindset, clear-thinking, and a smart strategy, you can get through this current crisis, as well as any and all future crises. I can say this with confidence because many, many business owners have done so.

During the recession of 2008, when whole industries seemed to be collapsing, some companies managed to survive, and even thrive, as a result of smart leadership. Some of these companies had the odds stacked against them.

Global consultancy Bain & Company analyzed nearly 3,900 companies to determine why some thrive during an economic downturn while others flounder, focusing in particular on the time immediately before and after the 2008 recession.

Their conclusion is that the biggest losers during the recession "tried to slash and burn their way to the other side, under the misconception that extreme cost-cutting would stabilize the enterprise...Still others tolerated poor results during the downturn, waiting to see what would happen, and then finally took action—too late."

The winners, on the other hand, were wise about taking advantage of opportunities. As the report indicates, "While they focused intensively on cost containment, [the winners] also looked beyond cost. Playing offense almost always trumps simply hunkering down, and the best companies usually gain market share during a challenging economy...The strongest companies coming out of recessions went on offense early while others thought only about survival."[5] Consider a large professional services company like Accenture. At a time when many companies are making bleak projections about the

---

[5] "Companies well-prepared for an economic downturn grew at 17 percent compared to zero growth among the losers," *Bain & Company*, May 16, 2019, https://www.bain.com/about/media-center/press-releases/2019/winning-in-a-downturn/

future, Accenture seems to have a much better outlook.

This is particularly impressive considering the fact that Accenture is full of consultants who regularly travel to meet with clients. How are they handling the current crisis when travel is highly restricted (if not banned altogether)? How are they able to help their clients through the turmoil?

By leaning into the opportunities presented by the lack of travel. According to Accenture CEO Julie Sweet, "We are deeply experienced in working virtually and already have deployed at scale, in the normal course of our business, the collaboration technologies and infrastructure for remote working...We are using our deep experience of working together virtually across Accenture and with our clients to help adapt how we work together."[6]

As a result, they have been able to rapidly ramp up the number of people working remotely from home.

By leaning into the crisis and looking for opportunities, many companies in many industries are able to thrive in circumstances that destroy others.

Wells Fargo, a company that sells financial products, would seem to be particularly susceptible to a recession, yet they have survived a number of economic downturns. In 2008, when banks were going under, Wells Fargo kept things simple, focused on what worked, and remained successful.

Proctor and Gamble thrived during the Great Depression of the 1930s through a counterintuitive

---

[6] Stuart Lauchlan, "Accenture CEO Julie Sweet," *Diginomica*, March 20, 2020, https://diginomica.com/accenture-ceo-julie-sweet-how-were-dealing-coronavirus-and-how-its-impacting-our-clients-needs

marketing strategy. When most companies were scaling down their advertising efforts, P&G actively pursued new marketing opportunities. Indeed, in 1933, they came up with the wild idea to produce a daily radio serial to promote their soap products. That program, called *Oxydol's Own Ma Perkins*, became the first "soap opera."[7]

While other business leaders were sticking their heads in the sand, Proctor & Gamble made smart decisions and kept pushing forward, looking for improvements they could make and actions they could take. As a result, they benefited tremendously. Similarly, FedEx, General Motors, and Apple are all companies that rose to prominence during recessionary periods.

Retail companies were hit especially hard during the 2008 recession, yet Amazon saw sales rise by 25

---

[7] Ethan Trex, "5 Great Depression Success Stories," *Mental Floss*, February 10, 2009, https://www.mentalfloss.com/article/20837/5-great-depression-success-stories

percent. While other companies retreated, Amazon moved into new markets and launched the next iteration of one of their most successful products: the Kindle 2.

On top of that, they focused even more strongly on customer service and competitive dominance, lowering prices at a time when customers were concerned about their income.[8]

As a consultant, you're not a retailer, but like Amazon, you can think about new offers, products, ideas, and services that will contribute to growth even during difficult times. Focus more strongly on meeting the particular needs your ideal clients are struggling with right now, lean into the chaos with

---

[8] Bobbie Johnson, "Amazon busts through recession with profit surge," *The Guardian*, October 22, 2009, https://www.theguardian.com/technology/2009/oct/23/amazon-profits

help and hope, and clients will be far more likely to respond.

Bain & Company's co-author on their research, Tom Holland, put it even more succinctly: "Think of a recession as a sharp curve on a race track—it's the best place to pass competitors, but requiring more skill than on a straightaway"[9]

Don't Bury Your Head in the Sand

Wells Fargo, P&G, and Amazon are not consultancy businesses. However, the basic mindset is the same in any industry. In difficult times, some leaders cross their fingers and hope for the storm to pass quickly, while others strategize and keep moving forward.

---

[9] "Companies well-prepared for an economic downturn grew at 17 percent compared to zero growth among the losers," Bain & Company, May 16, 2019, https://www.bain.com/about/media-center/press-releases/2019/winning-in-a-downturn/

Some scale back advertising, put their plans on hold, and hope for the best, while others make the most of what lies before them.

Remember, hope isn't a strategy, and burying your head in the sand won't get you anywhere. All it will do is cause opportunity to pass you by, and that coarse sand is really rough on the eyes!

Instead of hunkering down or hesitating to push forward, we strongly encourage you to look for growth opportunities right now. They're all around you, even in the midst of an economic downturn.

In her recent book *Seeing Around Corners*, corporate consultant and Columbia Business School professor Rita McGrath talks about the paradigmatic shifts in the business landscape that she calls *inflection points* which create new entrepreneurial opportunities.

As she explained to me on a recent call, "What an inflection point does, at its core, is change the taken-for-granted assumptions we've been making about our lives. Many of us are used to watching sports as part of our routine, but suddenly there are no sports happening anywhere in the world. A core part of many people's lives, which they assumed would always be there, has been taken away."

In a business context, the current crisis may be changing the business model that we're all used to. The ways we get paid, the ways we conduct meetings, the ways we connect with clients—so many things might be different now and in the future. The key, Rita says, is identifying these inflections points and using them to create a competitive advantage.

"This situation is going to produce remarkable opportunities," she continued. "Anytime there's an economic downturn, there's also a big rebound afterwards. Set yourself up to capitalize on that right now by searching for and identifying opportunities that are going to take your business higher."

Your focus makes all the difference. Don't liquidate your investments and head for the hills. Make it a priority to take action every day to build your business instead of withdrawing. Move forward instead of stepping back. Act wisely, but act boldly.

Even if the current crisis gets significantly worse, a complete shutdown of all businesses is highly unlikely—or, at least, won't last very long—which means companies are still going to need expertise and support. Many of them are trying to navigate uncharted waters right now.

If anything, they need your help more than ever. Figure out what impact the current situation is having on your ideal clients and infuse that into your positioning and messaging.

37

Later in the book, we'll look at some specific actions you can take during times of uncertainty, but if you don't get your thinking right, you won't see the steps you need to take to grow.

To use another well-known quote from Tony Robbins: "Where focus goes, energy flows."

Stay Positive and Healthy

It's not always easy to stay focused on the positive when you're being inundated with bad news and "doom and gloom" predictions about economic chaos. Do what you can to counteract the negative.

Don't become sedentary. Your physical health is more important than ever, so stay active. When you're physically fit, you feel better, and that helps you to think more clearly. Regardless of your situation, find ways to exercise. If you're stuck at home, do pushups and sit-ups right there. If you can get outside, take a walk or ride a bike. Enjoy the fresh air.

Of course, your brain is part of your body, so you also need to keep your mind sharp. It's time to study, up your game, and sharpen your sword. Use times of uncertainty to master new skills and get better.

Remember, your position in the market, and in the eyes of your clients, never stays still. You're either increasing demand and becoming more relevant or you're headed down the hill as you become less desirable.

Push past the metaphorical roadblock and keep moving forward.

Think of it this way: a time of crisis gives you the perfect chance to model the mindset that you want your current and future clients to have. Therefore, remain calm, be patient, make thoughtful decisions, but, above all, *take action*.

Right now, there's a good chance that many of your competitors are drawing back in fear, so it's the perfect time to step up and be a leader. Grab the steering wheel and keep your foot on the gas. Learn, improve, grow, take advantage of opportunities, and make decisions with confidence.

3

Staying Afloat & Managing the Now

To be clear, I am not recommending that you act naively during a time of pandemic and economic turmoil. Far from it.

On the contrary, acting boldly means taking some steps to mitigate the risk, even as you look for opportunities.

Trim the Fat

First, I recommend cutting all non-essential expenses. If it's not creating value in your life or business, get rid of it or reduce it drastically. Now is the time to focus your resources on those things that provide value and ROI.

A good way to begin doing this is to review your credit card bills. Examine the things that you are spending money on. Anything on that list that doesn't provide value should be cut—at least, for the time being.

You can revisit these items once the current uncertainty has passed, but you may find that you can continue to do without them. In that sense, the current crisis might be doing you a huge favor of revealing some fat you should trim from your business.

Ask for Discounts

Second, as part of that process, look at all of the products and services you use to run your business and determine which of those services are necessary. Of the necessary services, contact your suppliers and partners and ask them for flexible payment terms or a discount. Many of them will say yes and will be willing to work with you to keep your business

After all, they are trying to adjust to the same uncertainty as you, and offering a discount is more advantageous for them than losing you as a client. This process can add up to hundreds, if not thousands, of dollars in savings.

What Not to Cut

There are a few things that I'd encourage you *not* to cut, even in times of economic uncertainty. Actually, you might need them more than ever. This includes your marketing and advertising budgets, learning resources such as books, and the coaches you are working with.

It also includes the individuals and communities that support you, hold you accountable, and will help you grow your business in uncertainty. None of us can do this alone. We need people to help, support, encourage, and teach us.

If you're not already part of a supportive community that can provide resources, encouragement, and ideas, join one—or even create one.

As Rita McGrath said, "Find ten to fifteen people who you think are smart and who are willing to give maybe an hour a week for a virtual chat. Support each other. Share individual experiences. It can just be informal mingling, but that kind of regular communication is critical for consultants, especially if you're more on the independent side."

All of these people and resources will help keep you on your feet and moving in the right direction. When the status quo is shaken, learning resources can prevent you from becoming timid and complacent, so you're able to continue getting things done. Your marketing, books, and coaches (as long as they are creating value) are worth keeping.

Remember, if you're going to stay afloat, you need to be generating business now. Timid, fearful businesses are *less likely* to weather an economic downturn.

I'm not suggesting that you make reckless decisions. Rather, I am encouraging you to focus your efforts on those things that will keep you moving forward. It's time to get creative and embrace innovation. Now is a good time to try new offers, a new hook, or a different angle.

Think about what you've been doing up to this point. Break it down into various pieces and think about new and creative ways to deliver your services, offerings, and marketing. Any resource that can help you think in new directions will be worth the continued investment.

Virtual Workshops and Webinars

In this time of social distancing, virtual workshops and webinars provide a perfect way to hone your skills and learn new tactics even though you might be geographically limited.

Recently, I spoke with marketing and strategy consultant Dorie Clark, and she said, "Everyone is going to emerge from this situation knowing how to use Zoom and Skype very well. People are more interested in remote communication. They see the value in it, which means we finally have the potential of realizing the promise of a truly global client base. There are only so many people who will pay to fly you to Singapore or some other country to do consulting work with them in person, but plenty of people are willing to Zoom with you remotely, whether they're in Singapore, Australia, Brussels, or wherever. The dynamics are shifting."

If you're creative about it, there is always a way to get together with your clients. It may take some adjustment as you shift more from in-person meetings to virtual meetings.

As Dorie said, "Humans have evolved to socialize in person. It feels better, it feels easier, and it's a very intuitive thing to do, but we have to learn how to socialize virtually. We have to train ourselves to get comfortable with the mechanics of it."

Have you ever experienced an awkward virtual meeting? We can all relate.

Dorie continued, "There are some simple things newbies struggle with that can make virtual meetings a lousy experience. For example, where are you supposed to look? When we're speaking to someone in person, we know to look at their eyes or their face. However, in a virtual meeting, newbies will look down, they'll look at the screen, they'll stare off somewhere. They might not be not sure where the camera is. It just doesn't feel like a natural experience. We're all going to have to learn how to make the experience more comfortable and sophisticated."

John Warrillow, bestselling author of *Built to Sell: Creating a Business That Can Thrive Without You*, told me something similar: "These things are better done in person, but you can do them virtually in a way that is effective, efficient, and inexpensive. Business owners crave social interaction. We all miss that aspect of being in the office, which is why so many are conducting house parties and cocktail parties over

48

Zoom. It's the perfect time to offer a master class or virtual mastermind group—not just for the expertise you can share about the current situation but to meet the need to socialize."

There are a few things you can do to make a virtual meeting feel more natural. Try to remove distractions in the background, work in a quiet room (if possible, under the circumstances) with good lighting, and dress well. A virtual meeting will probably be more casual than an in-person meeting in an office setting, but you still want to make a good impression.

When speaking to people, look into the camera (not at the screen) and address them directly, as if you were in person. Avoid distracting body language. It helps if the camera is at eye level. Make sure you have a good microphone so people can hear you clearly. Call on people by name and get them involved.

If someone isn't participating, they might feel awkward speaking up in a virtual setting, so help them take that step. "Hey, So-and-so, what is your opinion about this subject? I know you have some experience with it."

Remote Coaching Sessions

Just because you're stuck at home doesn't mean you can't conduct coaching or advisory sessions. Offer remote coaching. These sessions can be either paid or free but will plant seeds for potential long-term relationships, and those relationships are more important than ever when people are anxious.

People tend to lean on those who have proven themselves as someone they can count on and trust, so if you provide value in a time of crisis, clients will be more likely to turn to you down the road.

Don't assume that people won't want to meet. Actually, they probably need the reassurance which makes it the perfect time for advisory work. After all, one of our greatest challenges as consultants is knowing what our ideal clients are thinking. Right now, everyone is thinking about the same thing, so you can tailor your messaging, make it timely, and it is sure to resonate with many, many people.

Stand on the Front Line

Personally, I am committed to helping my clients stay focused and optimistic. We've tightened our support, providing more check-ins so we can stay informed about how people are doing.

Through a series of LinkedIn posts, informative emails that provide concrete actions and recommendations, as well as regular virtual workshops, office hours and webinars, I am continually creating value for my clients by addressing the changing situation.

These are ways I help ensure that my clients are still making progress in their businesses, and they also keep our business top of mind.

Our virtual meetings have also created an excellent environment for clients to share ideas with one another. The collective experiences and shared advice have strengthened a sense of community and support among our clients.

As growth consultant Josh Long put it, "In your messaging, you need to provide certainty that you can help people navigate through this…So many business owners are like Chicken Little—they think the sky is falling. They're preparing for everything to blow up in their faces, for everyone to cancel everything and all business to stop. You can be the voice that says, 'Wait. Just wait. Be calm. Be patient.' You can be like

William Wallace in *Braveheart* telling everyone, 'Stand your ground.'"

I like that image. Yes, stand on the front line. Be visible. Be proactive, sharing the positive things: new ideas, strategies, and perspectives.

Remember, right now your clients are being inundated by various news media, and all of the stories are about the terrifying, impending *unknowns*. You can be a voice of reason and a source of certainty for your clients. Be the *known* amidst the *unknowns*.

Think about the information you can share right now that clients will find valuable. For example, I spoke with a consultant who works in the advertising industry. Many of her clients are having to lay off workers because they operate in industries that have been heavily impacted by the pandemic.

However, she recently learned about a huge new opportunity for advertisers selling to the government. She was able to share this timely information with her clients, guiding them in the best way to take advantage of the opportunity.

As Dorie Clark put it, "People are at home more, so they are consuming more content. In particular, they're very hungry for content that will help them navigate this situation. For that reason, I have doubled down on my newsletter and LinkedIn posts. I'm doing LinkedIn Live broadcasts. I'm just trying to find ways to reach out to people with helpful content, while also continuing to build my platform during this time so that I will have more people I can communicate with when the world is back in buying mode."

You're not limited to sharing only the content you've created yourself. You can also stay top of mind with your ideal clients by sharing a wide variety of relevant articles, resources, and content that other experts have created.

The point is, there are plenty of ways to share helpful content with clients and potential clients, even if we all continue to be stuck at home for a while longer. Start brainstorming ideas right now.

What creative approaches can you embed into your offerings to provide a lot of value to clients and potential clients? Meet them where they are! If they're stuck at home and scattered all over the world, you can still find creative ways to add value as long as you're willing to be innovative.

However you approach it, I recommend using multiple channels so you can reach people in different ways. Many companies are pulling back from social media. They're making fewer posts, publishing fewer articles, creating fewer videos. That creates both a massive *need* and a growing *opportunity*, so make the most of it.

Are People Buying?

It's easy to say your clients need you now more than ever, but if no one is buying, you're going to have a hard time keeping your business going.

So, what are the actual experiences of consultants these days? Are clients buying? To get a sense of how business is going during the current pandemic, I spoke to a number of people. One of those individuals, Perry Marshall, one of the world's leading marketing experts, noted an interesting trend.

"Recently, I conducted an office-hour Zoom call for my round table members," he said. "It was a Friday afternoon, and under normal circumstances, I'd be lucky to get a fourth of my clients to attend a conference call at that time. However, because of the current circumstances, three-fourths of my clients were present on the call. Everybody was paying attention, and they were all very involved in the discussion."

As Perry pointed out, people don't have fewer problems now than they did a few months ago—they have *more*. His advice?

"As Warren Buffet likes to say, 'Only when the tide goes out do you discover who's been swimming naked.' Right now, maybe 80 percent of your clients are swimming naked, meaning they are struggling at this time. What are you going to do about it? As I told one of my clients, 'You know more about lead generation, lead flow, sales follow-up. Even if those things aren't your main offerings, you can find ways to apply your expertise to add value at this time, so get on the phone and start calling your clients. Ask them how they're doing, and they will start sharing their problems. Then it's time to roll up your sleeves and get to work solving those problems.'"

Josh Long was even more upbeat. As he told me, "There are trillions of dollars flowing around right now. Yes, some companies and sectors are impacted badly by the current situation, but others are growing like crazy because of it."

John Warrillow adds an important point. "There's a distinction between income and having money. Right now, many of your clients may not have a lot of income because they don't have contracts coming in. However, especially in a B2B context, many businesses are coming off the best ten years of their lives. The smart ones will have socked away a few shekels for a downturn. Since more money will be harder to make for the time being, you have to prove that your services are an investment worth making, not an extra cost."

Help Clients Manage the Changes

Many organizations aren't working in the office right now, and their executives might not know how to be productive when working from home. Kids and pets are running around and making noise, they've got all kinds of distractions, and the whole home environment doesn't feel like a workplace.

It might seem like they've entered a whole new arena. Likewise, their employees are scattered about, and they are probably still trying to figure out how to work well together when they're not in the same room (and maybe not even in the same city or country).

Sales strategist Jill Konrath mentioned this adjustment during a recent call. "People are still trying to get settled into their home offices. They're trying to figure out how to get work done when everyone is dispersed. There's still chaos. They hope that there will be a finite end to this, but the ramifications of doing business under these conditions are huge."

As an outside expert, you may be able to provide key advice that will help them manage these changes and still get work done. At the same time, you will need to be very flexible when scheduling and speaking with clients.

We don't know how events are going to unfold in the future, and things may change faster than we would like. Be prepared to adjust on the fly.

As Jill Konrath said, "People tend to stay with the status quo unless they absolutely have to change, but it is imperative that consultants be willing to do some things differently and help clients adjust to future changes as they unfold."

Make Contact Now

While clients are dealing with downtime, lack of options, and anxiety about their businesses, you can provide key advice and encouragement to help them keep going. Now is a time to become *more* relevant, to create more demand for your expertise.

Use social media to gauge interest and make offers that are mindful of circumstances. Use your email list to reach out to existing clients or prospects. Don't be afraid to call people directly. Many will appreciate the human contact during this time.

As Dorie Clark said, "If you're in a position where you need business now, then you have to focus on sales, and that means doing something that is, frankly, a bit uncomfortable and possibly nerve-wracking. You're going to have to call your contacts."

She put it very bluntly: "It's like hand-to-hand combat! You have to get out there and 'work the Rolodex' because clients are more likely to hire you right now than strangers. The people who will hire you in a time like this are those people who already know you and trust you, people who have enough of a connection with you that they are willing to share their actual challenges."

We encourage you to reach out to *every client*, past and present, during this time to see how they're doing. They will appreciate the concern, and you can use it as a chance to offer support. If they're not ready to buy, don't be pushy. Just let them know that you are available to help at any time. Continue to reach out periodically.

Recently, I spent time on a Saturday morning calling each of my clients and checking on them. I didn't sell anything. Actually, I didn't talk business at all.

Instead, I just asked how they were doing and how their families were holding up, and they were very appreciative of my concern. Building relationships with your clients is always time well spent.

As Dorie put it, "Just check in and see how they're doing. Don't fool them with a sales pitch. Nobody likes that. Be thoughtful and upfront. If they have a problem you can help with, mention that you specialize in it. You might say, 'Hey, I just happen to offer this particular solution. If you know of anyone who needs it right now, I'd love to help, and I would appreciate a connection or referral.' As long as you're straight up about that and you have a good relationship with these people—and you're not cold-pitching random strangers—it will probably be well-received."

Josh Long said, "Many of our clients are nervous and need encouragement. I see myself as a kind of first responder in their businesses. When they are shaken up by something, we're there for them. Many of them are at capacity. They've reached their limit in the number of negative stimuli they can withstand and the number of potential problems they can process. In many cases, clients aren't being hit as hard as they think they are, but bad news, cancellations, and fears about the future make them believe they're in trouble. I'm telling everybody who is in a non-critically-affected business to put Coronavirus out of mind completely. Just look at your actual performance and see how you're doing. You might be doing better than you feel like you're doing."

Josh makes an important point here. Fears about the broader crisis can color the way we feel about the performance of our business. You may not be doing as badly as you think. The same goes for your clients. They might feel like their whole world is crashing down when, in fact, they are weathering the circumstances fairly well.

To counteract these feelings, I recommend looking at the real numbers and encouraging your clients to do the same. Compare your results over the last two or three months against where you were last year. Look at sales, new clients, revenue, and cancellations. Ignore the hype and fear and see what the actual numbers tell you.

Guide your clients through a similar process. They might be surprised at what the actual numbers reveal about their businesses.

Not long ago, Josh had a client who panicked because he had eight cancellations in a single day for his landscape business.

"Coronavirus is killing all of my business," the client said.

Josh stepped in and helped him look at the actual data. As it turned out, he'd lost more clients during the same month the previous year, long before the pandemic was even a glimmer in anyone's eye.

Further breaking it down, it turned out that four of this year's cancellations were due to the weather, and only two of them were related to pandemic-inspired downsizing. The current crisis had made a far smaller impact on his business than he thought.

In reality, his landscaping business was performing better than it had the year before. He was still growing. Fear had made him unable to see it until the actual numbers revealed the truth.

Chasing the first responder metaphor, Josh continued, "It's our job to run toward our clients. Step into their situations and start offering help. For example, let's say you have a client who canceled their pay-per-click advertising because of the current uncertainty. You have access to their analytics, so take a look and see what you can find. Are more people navigating to a certain page? Is there a set of leads they need to overcommunicate? See what the data reveals and write copy for messaging to help them get more out of their advertising. Think like an innovator and find creative solutions. Keep the relationship alive by helping clients continue to grow."

Adjust Your Payment Terms

If someone does decide to buy, we recommend providing all payment terms upfront so you get paid in advance for the work you do before you start. Remember, we're being bold, but we're also being wise about uncertainty.

Don't assume things can't get worse for a client, industry, or the economy as a whole. That's not a reason to crumble in fear. That's just a reason to take a few reasonable precautions. Of course, a client might not be able to pay everything upfront, so it's okay to be flexible, depending on your relationship with the client.

Josh Long encourages reducing the engagement risk for clients by changing the time horizon.

"When the market is scared, wallets get tight because people are afraid they're going to lose their last dollar," he said. "Maybe frame the work into bite-sized chunks of time. Instead of selling a whole package that lasts six months and costs $40,000, sell two weeks at a time, with a $2,000 payment at the beginning of each. Also, consider adding a money-back guarantee. *De-risk the relationship.*"

Down-sell Your Clients

On a similar note, Dorie Clark recommends that you consider down-selling a client rather than losing them entirely. As she shared with me, she had a client who had expressed interest in a strategy session, but over a single weekend, she lost 40 percent of her business.

Suddenly, she could no longer afford the strategy session. Dorie recommended a more affordable online program as an alternative. It was something that the client needed, and something she could handle under the circumstances.

If necessary, recalibrate your services, offering things that your clients can afford under the circumstances in order to maintain the relationship. While you may have a typical fee that you charge for a project, try offers at both lower and higher fee levels.

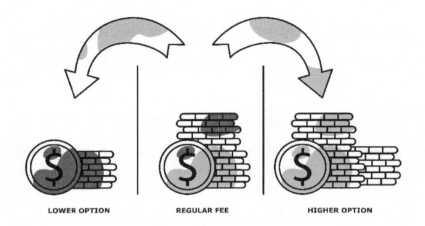

LOWER OPTION   REGULAR FEE   HIGHER OPTION

Your clients need what you have to offer. Reach out, make connections, and continue growing your business—as much, if not more, than ever before.

In a wide-scale crisis, some business leaders freeze up, and their businesses die as a result. You don't have to be one of them. Your forward actions will keep you moving up as others move down.

4

Planting Seeds to Thrive

It bears repeating: in times like these, lean into your existing clients. They are feeling anxious about the future, so make sure they're healthy and doing well. If you haven't reached out in a while, now is the perfect opportunity.

As this crisis continues to unfold, spend more time with them, provide encouragement, and help them weather the storm. They hired you in the first place for your expertise, so use it now in their time of need. In the process, you will be planting seeds for long-term growth well beyond the current circumstances.

We're following our own advice. We've opened additional office hours so we can provide more coaching to clients. That's in addition to our regular weekly community call and one-on-one coaching calls. We make sure to stay in touch with every client personally to see how they're doing. It's a small act of kindness, and it shows that we're concerned about their well-being.

Your clients need to know that they can count on you, even in a time of social distancing. As we said before, don't be afraid to go through your client list and touch base with every single person. Ask how they're doing—they will appreciate it. More than that, they need it. They need to know that you genuinely care about their well-being.

Negative thinking often grows and festers in isolation, so strengthen those relationships. Prove yourself. Show that you're there for them. It should always be your goal to provide the highest level of personal support for your clients, and they really need encouragement right now.

Be a Little Bolder

As Perry Marshall pointed out, your approach might have to be a little bolder these days. He has a consulting client who runs advertising for a company that installs equipment in schools. Recently, the owner of the company said, "With these quarantines going on, schools are not going to let us come on the property and install equipment."

However, the equipment is necessary and perhaps even more helpful in the current crisis, so Perry told his client, "Don't try to convince the terrified company owner to call the school. *You* get on the phone, call the school, and ask on his behalf. Tell the school, 'I have someone who needs to install important equipment at your school. What safety or health checklists do they need to follow?' In other words, pave the way for your clients."

In a sense, as Perry put it, "Because people are fearful, you almost have to ask forgiveness instead of permission for solving their problems."

Reaching New Clients

While much of your business during economic uncertainty is likely to come from existing clients, people who already trust you because you've proven yourself, that doesn't mean you shouldn't also continue trying to reach new people.

Though it might be a little more difficult than usual, you can build trust with new and potential buyers while working remotely. How do you this? One way you do it is through your existing clients.

Martin Lindstrom, one of the world's foremost business and culture transformation experts, shared this advice:

"You can't ask people to trust you, but you can ask others to offer first-hand impressions of you, convey their trust in you, and share their experiences in dealing with you. Of course, this can't look, and shouldn't come across, as manufactured. It has to be very natural and sincere."

He also recommends using this time to do charity work through your business by using your skills to prove that what you do has an impact on the world. Contribute to causes that people really need right now.

As Martin put it, "If you give, share, and help others, and due to your efforts, they express their gratitude, trust will be developed. Again, trust doesn't come by you claiming it. It comes through the voices of others."

This is a time where the reputation you've built through the work, help, and wisdom you've provided can translate into meaningful testimonials that will help your business continue to grow. Now is a time to prove yourself, so work hard to *earn* the praise that will attract new clients.

At the same time, you can, and should, reach out directly to your ideal clients. The services and support you offer now can bridge gaps and create new relationships that will bear fruit both now and, even more, after the crisis has passed.

Plus, when you speak to people directly, the conversations will reveal the specific problems potential clients are facing and the kinds of help they're looking for, which can give you ideas for improving the services you provide.

Don't Be Afraid to Pivot

Bear in mind, depending on your industry, you may have to pivot a bit in the services you provide. One of Perry Marshall's big revenue generators is a seminar they run, which was planned for May 27 in Chicago. With everything being shut down, it is unlikely that the seminar will occur. At best, it will get moved to August, and it might become a virtual seminar.

Instead of fighting this reality, Perry has accepted it and pivoted. "Nobody is thinking about the seminar right now, so instead of pushing it anyway, we're looking at how we can help our clients with the problems that are occupying their minds right now."

To do that, he is devoting more time than ever to contacting his clients individually and seeing what they need. In that way, he has become even more visible than ever.

Making your personal brand visible is very important during this time or at any time of crisis. Not only will it help you generate more business, but you can plant seeds for future business. More than that, you position yourself as an authority, someone that people can turn to when the status quo has been threatened.

Produce Relevant Content

Beyond contacting clients individually, it's a great time to post relevant content on social media. Provide value through posts, articles, videos, podcasts, guides, and checklists. As I said earlier, offer free or paid webinars and send out newsletters. Consider finally writing that amazing book you've been thinking about for a while.

Some of these can actually provide passive revenue streams to mitigate a downturn in client sales. This has been Dorie Clark's experience.

"I can handle things being a little slower right now," she said, "because I have revenue coming in regardless of what I'm doing thanks to passive income streams I've set up with online courses and royalties for books I've written over the years."

A good way to reach out to your ideal clients is to invite them onto your podcast if you have one. Or even if you don't have one, offer to interview them on their area of expertise. You can then use that content for articles and videos.

It's a mutually beneficial outreach that creates a point of contact which might lead to an ongoing relationship. Find other ways to add value to your ideal clients. Don't be afraid to ask directly if there are any ways you can help them.

It's a good time to write articles, so reach out to trade publications and pitch them a few ideas. They're always looking for relevant content, but they may have temporarily lost some of their regular sources.

Staff writers or regular contributors might not be as available as they were because of changing circumstances, but publications still need the ad revenue they generate from regular content, and they still need to provide value to their audience or association members.

You can step into the gap and fill a need. When you contact publications, don't just offer your writing services. Instead, to prove that you have value to give, suggest one to three specific relevant or timely topics that you could write articles about, and mention the expertise or experience that qualifies you to write on these topics.

Beyond writing articles, you might also consider hosting free webinars on the publication's website.

Use the Quiet Time Productively

If you have more quiet time than usual because of the chaos, use the time to work on your business. Of course, it's entirely possible that you'll be so busy delivering value to clients that you won't have nearly as much quiet time as you might expect.

Still, when you have a chance, take some time to work on the internal parts of your business, so you can set stronger foundations, develop your intellectual property, and establish your authority. Study, plan, write, record video, post on social media, reach out— make the most of this time.

When you're busy delivering for your clients, you don't always have enough time to work on your business, so this is the perfect time to do it. Appreciate the opportunity that has been presented to you and run with it.

By staying busy, you will be at an advantage, because many people allow themselves to become paralyzed by fear of the unknown. Instead of cowering at home, holding back, or simply waiting for the news to get better, capitalize on the opening in the marketplace. There's less noise out there right now, so your content will stand out.

5

What's Next?

What does the future hold? Nobody can say for sure, but our current crisis is likely to continue for a while as governments and healthcare experts try to get a handle on it. The long-term economic impact will only become clear over time, but there's a very good chance that we may enter a recession. For this reason, it's important to create a lean and profitable business model.

We run our business lean for this very reason. With no big overhead or high costs to run our team, we are able to survive and thrive in the midst of economic downturns that can cripple small businesses. Don't wait until your business is suffering. Dial in the right business model now so you're ready for whatever happens.

Remember, chaos is not the status quo. When hard times hit, sometimes people assume they are entering a new normal, and they begin to despair. On the other hand, when things are going well, those same people often assume the good times will continue to roll on forever.

The truth is, chaos is cyclical. It comes and goes. It would be fair to say that the only sure thing for entrepreneurs is uncertainty.

In the Middle of Chaos Theory

Will there be long-term consequences of the current pandemic? Most likely. As Perry Marshall put it, "There are going to be more disruptions to the way consultants do business. We're in the middle of chaos theory right now. We're already seeing restaurants and schools shutting down, and more businesses are likely to follow. Systems are going to become overloaded."

John Warrillow pointed out the long-term damage to commercial real estate as more businesses shift to remote work. "A lot of people will come through this crisis and think, 'We were pretty productive working from home. Maybe we don't need that $5,000-a-month office space."

Accept all of these things not as reasons to fear. Find ways to maintain a positive mindset.

As Perry continued, "Anything could break anywhere at any time, but don't run away from the chaos! Lean into it. Yesterday, I tried to conduct a GoToWebinar meeting, but the website was having trouble, so we had to move to Zoom. Then we were having trouble with Zoom, so we moved to the old-fashioned conference call. We have to accept that anything can break at any time, but instead of running away from it, we get creative about dealing with it."

Looking at the larger point, Perry said, "Wherever there is chaos, there is opportunity. People need help right now, so put yourself out there and be proactive. See what your clients need right now, pivot if necessary, and help them."

Fortunately, chaos doesn't mean there's absolutely no order or structure. As Perry explained, "I'll tell you how chaos works. There are predictable patterns to it.

There are ways that you can react to it if you're willing to pivot."

Jill Konrath compares the current situation to past economic crises, and she's not afraid to mince words about the long-term consequences. "There will be more layoffs. There will be fewer people in the corporate offices that consultants call on, and those people will be overwhelmed with work as they try to pick up the slack. Like the 2008 recession, all sorts of people will move from just doing their work to suddenly being swamped, which means change of any sort will become extraordinarily difficult for them. As a result, they will become more likely to find a status quo and stick to it."

Even so, Jill doesn't despair. She has been through many ups and downs in the market. During the 2000 recession, she lost 90 percent of her clients over the course of three months, but she hung in there and eventually bounced back. Her advice?

"Consultants must be prepared to do some things differently. Deepen your expertise in your field. Focus on learning more and getting more ideas. Look at the ways you can impact your existing client base during this time. Take a look at the problems your typical clients are facing now and start thinking about how you can solve them. Consider creating a low-risk project to help them. It might have to be low risk because people won't want to make big decisions right now, especially with outside vendors."

She recommends approaching clients and saying, "With the current problems you're having—layoffs, struggling customers, or whatever the issue may be— I thought we might be able to help you out." Then propose a low-risk project that will help them.

She also recommends that you continue to try to attract new clients. If you're losing existing clients because of the chaos, don't assume they will come back. Having lost over 90 percent of her clients in 2000, she speaks from experience, so I asked her about the mindset that helped her recover from that setback.

"At first, I got into a negative mindset like everybody else, because we're all human. You get down on yourself and start questioning whether or not you're a viable consultant. You're scared. One day, I opened myself up to some other consultants. 'It's really tough,' I said. 'People aren't answering the phone. They're not responding to emails. I'm worried that I've lost my mojo.' And everyone else said, 'Yes, that's exactly what we're dealing with as well.' Suddenly, I realized, it wasn't just me. This is what everyone is facing. I wasn't losing my touch. We were *all* dealing with the same thing. That flipped a switch in my mind. *This is not a problem. It's a challenge.*"

Indeed, seeing the current crisis as a *challenge* changed her whole mindset. Suddenly, it was a thing to be overcome, a hurdle to jump over, not a reason to despair.

"Your brain loves a challenge," Jill said, "so open yourself up to new ideas."

In her case, she began researching and experimenting to find out what her clients and potential clients needed.

Her advice is, "Don't panic. People will hear the desperation in your voice. Do everything from a position of calmness."

Josh Long agreed. "Helping people get more focus and clarity so they can turn down the noise is a big opportunity. I like dealing with the mindset of my clients. It's the best lever if they're willing to tackle it."

Our response to uncertainty is, after all, a product of biology. As Josh continued, "The amygdala in your brain constantly senses fear and instills a fight-or-flight response, so look at how you can support your clients in the panic. Help them stop wringing their hands all the time. There's a huge opportunity in helping people stay sane. When they get punched in the gut and knocked down, what mindset will help them get back up?"

Dorie Clark shared something similar. "Reframe the situation for yourself and for your clients. Instead of viewing this as some terrible circumstance that has been thrust upon you, take a proactive viewpoint. A lot of things that we intended to do have been canceled, but we can look at it as a great time to focus. Treat it as a sabbatical. What would you do if this were a sabbatical? Maybe you would launch that web series you've been talking about."

Avoid a Lack of Inertia

There's always a challenge to be overcome, so make the most of the opportunities that are before you. Be ready for changes, and when others react with trepidation, continue making progress and taking action.

"When trouble strikes, some people turtle," John Warrillow said. "They cut expenses to the bone and try to ride it out. Others just freeze. They become catatonic. I believe forward momentum is better than nothing. Great things happen when you're in the market."

As he explained, "The worst enemy of consultants right now is not COVID-19 or even the economic impact it will inevitably produce. The worst enemy is *lack of inertia*...it's a very unique time to be a consultant because everybody is disrupted. Every

92

business model is under scrutiny, but as a consultant, you have the opportunity to make a huge impact."

"Some people are going to come through this crisis and realize it wasn't actually that bad," John Warrillow said. "Somehow, their business was still pretty productive, even though everyone was working from home."

As he reminded me, "I've lived through the tech wreck of the 90s, the economic fallout after 9/11, the 2008 recession. I owned businesses, including a consulting business, during all of them, and I am convinced that this, too, shall pass. Flash forward a year from now, and we will almost certainly have a vaccine for COVID-19. Hopefully, at some point soon, widespread testing will be underway. We are mobilizing an entire manufacturing sector to make ventilators and protective gear. People are taking action to self-isolate in order to stem the impact. It looks bad now, but we will get through this like we've gotten through all of the other bad times."

Boost Your Well-Being

Stay positive. Keep pushing forward. Take care of yourself and don't flee. As I mentioned earlier, one of the best ways you can maintain a positive mindset is by staying physically active. When you're active, your body releases endorphins, which contribute to your sense of well-being.

The science shows that regular exercise makes you feel more energetic throughout the day and enables you to sleep better at night. You're more relaxed, more positive about yourself, more resilient, and you have sharper memories. That, in turn, enables you to make clear-headed decisions, and it gives you the energy you need to keep moving

Regular exercise even has a profound effect on depression and anxiety, no matter your age or fitness level. You probably don't need as much activity as you think to enjoy the benefits. Just thirty minutes of moderate exercise five times a week is enough, so don't assume you need to devote hours at the gym or train for a marathon. [10]

It helps to pick a physical activity that you enjoy. Maybe you like running, or maybe you prefer riding your bike. Make a nice walk in the evening is your cup of tea, or perhaps you're just fine doing some aerobic exercise in your living room at home. Then again, you may actually be training for a marathon—that's great, too (and kind of impressive).

---

[10] Lawrence Robinson, Jeanne Segal, Ph.D., and Melinda Smith, M.A., "The Mental Health Benefits of Exercise," *HelpGuide*, June 2019, https://www.helpguide.org/articles/healthy-living/the-mental-health-benefits-of-exercise.htm

Leading in the Uncertainty

Though you may feel a bit like a deer in the headlights right now, the current climate of uncertainty is your opportunity to lead, make great strides in your business, and come out on top. Whatever the future holds, you can keep working and creating a prosperous future.

The best investments you can make during a time of trouble are *your business, your mindset, your family, your health*, and *your client relationships*. There is always a silver lining—choose to believe that and act accordingly.

Stay strong. Plant the right seeds now, and they will nourish you for years to come.

The key is to create the right plan, implement it, and work at it consistently. If you do, you will emerge from this crisis—and any future chaos or uncertainty—stronger than before. Not only will you survive, but you will also thrive.

Don't wait, don't despair, don't overthink—act! Your actions today create your future.

Clarity Coaching Program for Consultants

In the Clarity Coaching Program for Consultants, you'll learn the proven "Consulting Success® Framework" which focuses on optimizing all aspects of your consulting business, strategy, and marketing so you can reach your full potential as a consultant.

We've helped hundreds of consultants from around the world to optimize their messaging, business model and improve lead flow during the Clarity Program.

We have tested and developed a series of simple steps that support rapid learning and implementation to help you create real progress in your business.

The progress you make and strategy you'll develop translates to a solid consulting business foundation and increased revenue.

We teach you how to develop a powerful brand and a marketing system that attracts ideal clients and communicates greater value for your work.

To learn more visit www.consultingsuccess.com and click on "Coaching"

Momentum: The Proven Online Program to Quit Your Job and Become a Successful Consultant

Would you like to know what has enabled hundreds of people to quit their jobs and become high six- or seven-figure consultants with waiting lists of clients who are drawn to them almost magnetically?

Would you like to know what separates consultants who control their schedules, make a great impact doing what they're good at, and earn enough money to take time off and enjoy it with their families, traveling, golfing, skiing, or just lying on the beach...from consultants who work seventy to eighty hours a week just to pay the mortgage?

Would you like to know what separates a consultant who happily turns away potential clients because they're not the PERFECT fit…from a consultant who HAS to take every client they can get, regardless of how time-consuming and hair-pullingly irritating they will be because "beggars can't be choosers?"

The thing that separates them is pretty simple, actually. It's *having the right system and foundation in place.*

That system is Momentum: the proven implementation program for consultants to transition from employee to successful consultant.

Learn more at consultingsuccess.com/momentum

About the Author

Michael Zipursky is the CEO of Consulting Success®
and Coach to Consultants. He is a leading authority on
optimizing marketing, positioning, pricing and
business models for independent and small consulting
firms.

He has advised organizations like Financial Times,
Dow Jones, RBC, and helped Panasonic launch new
products into global markets, but more importantly,
he's helped over 370 consultants from around the
world in over fifty industries add six and seven figures
to their annual revenues.

His work has been featured in *Forbes, Entrepreneur, Marketing Profs, FOX Business,* among many other publications.

Over 35,000 consultants read his weekly consulting newsletter. Michael is also the author of the Amazon Bestsellers *The Elite Consulting Mind* and *Consulting Success®,* the book.

Made in the USA
Monee, IL
24 November 2020